Lucien Bé

THE MONT SAINT-MICHEL

Translated by : Angela Moyon

ÉDITIONS OUEST-FRANCE
13, rue du Breil, Rennes

Barnacle geese in the bay. (Photograph by André Mauxion)
The abbey seen from the south-east. (Photograph by Bertrand Dauleux)

Mont Saint-Michel seen from the south-west. (Photograph by Bertrand Dauleux)

Many writers have already tried to render the magic of Mont Saint-Michel. Madame de Sévigné wrote to her daughter in the following terms, "From my room, I could see the sea and Mont Saint-Michel, the haughty Mont that you have already seen standing proud, and that has seen you looking so beautiful". Victor Hugo thought that Mont Saint-Michel was to the sea what the pyramid of Keops is to the desert. Guy de Maupassant described it as "a sheer-sided abbey, rising in the distance, far from land, like an imaginary manorhouse, stupefying as a dream palace, improbably strange and beautiful." And Jules Michelet defined its charm, "It is not dry land yet it is not the sea".

The gift of land and sea

Sea is indeed part of the history, and beauty, of Mont Saint-Michel. Sometime in the dim and distant past, the sea invaded the bay, leaving only a few hillocks uncovered, resistant piles of granite or granulite, among them Mont Saint-Michel with a height of 260 ft., the island of Tombelaine, and Mont-Dol which is now far inland.

Then the sea ebbed, giving way to a forest traditionally thought to have been called the Scissy Forest. Gradually, over the centuries, the sea flowed back in again, covering the desolate landscape. For people living in those far-distant times, the scenery may have been very different to what we see today, but little is known about it. Folk memory is more especially concerned with tales of a tidal wave that was said to have put the Mont "in peril of the sea". One theory states that the forest was, for many years, protected by a coastal belt. When the sea suddenly broke through this last natural barrier, it surrounded the Mont.

The tidal range, i.e. the difference in levels between high and low tides, is particularly high at Mont Saint-Michel, indeed it is one of the highest in the world at more than 39 ft. As the surface of the Bay is almost flat, the sea ebbs over an enormous distance, and flows back in very quickly, at a speed of almost 13 m.p.h. Hence the superbly picturesque description of a tide flowing as quickly as a horse at the gallop, which tradition invented for the sea at Mont Saint-Michel.

There are three main rivers flowing into the Bay and meandering across the shore i.e. the Sée, Sélune and Couesnon. It is the latter that forms the boundary between Brittany and Normandy, so that Mont Saint-Michel, although so close to Brittany, is actually one of Normandy's major tourist attractions! Sometimes the rivers flow beneath the sand, creating dangerous quicksands, and the mist can also rise quickly, catching fishermen or walkers unawares.

Mont Saint-Michel rises above a shoreline that is, in some places, covered with grey mud known as sea sand. When the sea no longer covers the sand, maritime plants such as saltwort and sea fennel begin to grow. Beyond them are the salt meadows in which salt-marsh sheep so enjoy grazing.

In this setting of sand, sea and sky, an abbey was built to resemble a citadel, rising to a height of more than 550 ft. at the top of the spire on the church.

Mont Tombe and the hermits

It is because Mont Saint-Michel was so far off the beaten track for such a long time that, paradoxically, it became a centre of spirituality and art.

The Romans, who had occupied and transformed Gaul, left no marks on this hill. It was far away from the fine roads along which Roman traditions spread and far away from the main towns to which the Romans paid such attention. Yet the Mont may well have been the centre of pagan cults that were later ousted and replaced by Christianity.

With the spread of Christianity, the world underwent major change. Missionaries spread Christ's Word throughout the Roman Empire until, gradually, it became Christian, before breaking up under repeated attacks by the barbarians, invaders from the East. But they, like the Franks under Clovis, also turned to Christianity.

The abbey seen from the south-west. (Photograph by Bertrand Dauleux)

In those days, Mont Saint-Michel was called Mont Tombe, from the Celtic word *"tun"* meaning "hill" or from the Latin word *"tumba"* meaning "tomb". Christianity encouraged the most pious believers to leave their homes, families, and friends to live well away from urban centres in solitude and poverty (an idea that was diametrically opposed to the Roman ideal) and to pray to God. The Mont was an perfect setting for such hermits and it was they who built the first chapels there, one of them dedicated to St. Stephen and another to St. Symphorian. Legend has it that these pious Christians lit fires to pass messages to the inhabitants of Astériac, later Beauvoir. When the peasants saw the smoke, they would load food onto a donkey that was guided by the Hand of God to the doors of the hermits' retreats. A wolf that ate the ass was condemned by God to take over its work.

Mont Saint-Michel consecrated to St. Michael

Although this was an outstanding place, it had not yet been consecrated in an equally outstanding manner. St. Michael had begun to be the subject of veneration throughout the Christian world, in Asia Minor, Greece and Italy. According to the Biblical tradition, Michael was one of the archangels, with Raphael and Gabriel. When Satan, the fallen angel, argued with God, the Archangel had, in turn, argued with him, crying "Who is like God?", or *Mi-ka-el* in Hebrew. Through his action, he became the leader of the celestial army and Michael the Archangel was commonly associated with thunder and lightning, and tall, lonely mountains. He appeared in Monte Gargano, a spur of rock high above the Adriatic, and in Rome where the Hadrian Mausoleum became the Castel Sant'Angelo in memory of this vision.

In a world that was in turmoil after the collapse of the Roman Empire, the Bishops, confident in their role as spiritual leaders, provided the only unopposed authority in the towns. At the start of the 8th century, the Bishop of Avranches, a town near Mont Saint-Michel, was a man named Aubert. A later narrative tells how he dedicated the Mont to St. Michael after he had seen the Archangel in a dream and been ordered by Michael to build a chapel on the rock. Legend has it that the Archangel, in order to convince Aubert, pushed his finger into the disbelieving Bishop's skull. But this was not sufficient and the Archangel had to give further signs of his genuineness. A stolen bull was found at the top of the rock, as the Archangel had said. Aubert sent two messengers to Italy and Monte Gargano. They brought back a piece of the red mantle that St. Michael was wearing when he appeared in Italy, and a fragment of the altar on which he had set his foot. This created a link between the Italian sanctuary and the Mont. The French sanctuary was consecrated on 16th October 708 A.D; Mont Saint-Michel was born. When the messengers returned from Italy, they are said to have discovered a "new world where before their departure there had been only thick bushes". This is thought to indicate that the sea had completely, and suddenly, covered the forest. Meanwhile, Mont Saint-Michel had become a real island.

On the rock, there were only a few huts scattered across the area between the two chapels. Aubert decided to build a church. The site was indicated by yet another miracle. Dew fell and the new church was to be built on the area of earth that had remained dry. The Bishop called together the local peasants, so that the site could be cleared, and Heaven again came to Man's assistance. One of the inhabitants of the village of Huysnes had a vision. He left his house with his twelve sons and cleared an enormous rock off the land. Another legend tells how one of his children, who was then no more than a toddler, succeeded in moving the rock by giving it a slight push with his foot. Life would have been impossible, though, without drinking water. And, again by miracle, a spring was discovered at the foot of the rock; it is now known as St. Aubert's Spring.

Aubert installed clerks with responsibility for worshipping St. Michael. All that is thought to remain of the original church is the wall of huge stones called the "Cyclopean" wall in one of the crypts, the Chapel of Our-Lady-Underground.

The consecration of Mont Saint-Michel preceded a new era for the Western World. Another Empire, this time controlled by the Franks, was set up under the rule of Charlemagne, leading to political reorganisation and an intellectual renaissance.

Mont Saint-Michel seen from the west. (Photograph by Hervé Champollion)

The Duke of Normandy created the Benedictine abbey

The Carolingian renaissance, however, was soon under a new threat, this time from the sea, in the forms of annual invasions launched by men from the North, the Norsemen or Vikings, kings of the maritime world. They pillaged the church on Mont Saint-Michel in 847 A.D. Yet Aubert's disciples did not abandon their island, unlike many other monks who left monasteries in peril and carried the precious relics of their saints far inland.

The Vikings finally established a permanent settlement along the coast and on the banks of the R. Seine. In 911 A.D. Charlemagne's descendent, Charles the Simple, King of France, signed an agreement with the Viking Chief, Rolf or Rollo, known as the Treaty of Saint-Clair-sur-Epte. The Viking chieftain received the territory thereafter called "Normandy" but recognised the sovereignty of the King of France and was converted to Roman Catholicism. He also defended the men of the Church and imposed his law on all the other Normans. In 933 A.D., Rollo's son was granted the Cherbourg Peninsula and the Avranches District. In 942 A.D., Richard I, Rollo's grandson, became Chief of the Vikings, at the age of 10 years. Later, he was to show remarkable zeal with regard to the Normans' new faith, and he expressed a desire to raise the Church in his Duchy from its state of collapse.

There were still a number of Men of the Church on Mont Saint-Michel. Often they were described as canons. Yet they seemed to be rather too independent and they led a luxurious life that could scarcely be deemed to comply with Christian precepts. However, a major reform changed the Church. In 910 A.D., Cluny Abbey was founded and it offered a new way of life to men who devoted their existence to God, by implementing the Benedictine "Rule". This organisation of monastic life had been devised by St. Benedict of Nursia in 529 A.D. and modified by Benedict of Aniane in 817 A.D.

Richard I of Normandy held a meeting with the King of France, Lothar, on the banks of the R. Epte in 965 A.D. in order to ensure his political power. The Duke then decided to devote himself to religious reform and, in 966 A.D., he imposed the Benedictine Rule on Mont Saint-Michel. The older canons were evicted, as was the guardian of the relics who then hid the remains of St. Aubert. In their place, the Duke set up a community of Benedictines, each of them chosen from among the brothers who had originally come from Ghent and who had already succeeded in re-establishing the faith in Fontenelle, now Saint-Wandrille Abbey. Maynard was appointed as the Mont's first Abbot and soon the church itself was rebuilt. It is now a crypt, Our Lady Underground (*Notre-Dame-sous-Terre*).

The monastic community had, then, acquired a leader and a father, the Abbot, and he had total authority over the monks. Theoretically, they had the right to elect their Abbot but, in fact, the Dukes of Normandy often imposed their own candidate. The monks' duty was to pray for all other people, indeed for the whole of the society of which they formed the soul and which, in return, was obliged to provide them with their everyday needs.

Duke Richard II and William of Volpiano : the reform of the Church in Normandy

Richard II (996-1026) was the first to express his pleasure at being called "Duke of Normandy", and it was on Mont Saint-Michel that he married Judith, the daughter of Duke Conan of Brittany. The Duke of Normandy, like other illustrious visitors, indeed like all other Christians, was required to give the abbey gifts to extend its estate, for in feudal society, an abbey was a sort of collective domain. Although each monk was personally poor, the abbey could be wealthy and, by making its ceremonies more solemn and its buildings more beautiful, it could work to the glory of God.

The Forward Gate. (Photograph by Bertrand Dauleux)

The Boulevard Gate. (Photograph by Bertrand Dauleux)

The English bombards. (Photograph by Bertrand Dauleux)

Even though the Dukes had brought unity and peace to Normandy, conflict was still rife on its borders. At the request of Richard II, a Norwegian king came to pillage Dol and the Norse sagas contain a description of the battle that raged in the "round fjord", i.e. Mont Saint-Michel Bay.

Richard II encouraged further reform in the Roman Catholic Church in Normandy and, to this end, called upon William of Volpiano (962-1031). He was an Italian who had already reorganised a large number of abbeys before reaching Dijon and Burgundy to which he came at the invitation of Abbot Maïeul of Cluny. William then settled in Fécamp and set about reforming the monasteries in Normandy - St. Ouen's in Rouen, Bernay, Cerisy and Mont Saint-Michel. Thanks to his efforts, Normandy was to become the birthplace of countless Bishops and Abbots, all of them austere and knowledgeable.

William brought with him the influence of Cluny. The monks prayed at services, first and foremost the conventual Mass said in the presence of the entire community and personal Masses said for each of the monks. But the very number of services led to a need for specially-designed buildings including one main church and numerous chapels. This in turn meant that the architecture had to be audacious in size and complex in layout. The increased number of monks also led to a need for adequate accommodation. All this explains why William of Volpiano was so deeply interested in architecture and why his reform brought new buildings in its wake.

William's influence was maintained on the Mont through the members of his family or the followers that he imposed as Abbots.

An architectural challenge : the building of the Romanesque abbey

On Mont Saint-Michel, any building project involved a high degree of risk. Account had to be taken of the sheer-sided rock and its conical shape when trying to design a large church. But there was a sense of urgency for the previous buildings had been destroyed by fire in 992 A.D., an event said to have been foretold by the appearance of a comet. It took almost one hundred years to complete the Romanesque church. Our Lady Underground was given a vaulted roof, proof of new techniques and tastes. Then the crypt of Our Lady of the Thirty Candles (*Notre-Dame des Trente Cierges*) was built. It was designed to support the north side of the transept in the church above. As to St. Martin's Chapel, its rounded barrel vaulting supported the south arm of the transept.

The monks liked stone vaulted roofs because they improved the acoustics, an important feature of Gregorian chant.

The stability of the church was then guaranteed thanks to a skeleton of pillars and arches rather than by an accumulation of stones. Masonry had changed; it had become architecture. The inclusion of arches made it possible to build galleries and windows in order to provide the building with natural lighting. In those early days, the nave had seven spans. It stood high above the Mont and was completed in 1084. However, the north wall of the church collapsed on the monks' dorter one night in 1103, fortunately while the monks were at prayer in the church.

The Romanesque abbey was completed in the early years of the 12th century. The entrance was on the north-west side of the island. The abbey buildings had three storeys. Near the entrance, the monks welcomed pilgrims to the almonry, now called the Aquilon Chamber. Day-to-day life revolved around the buildings above, where there was the monks' gallery and the dorter, built on the same level as the church so that the monks could reach it more easily at night when they attended Matins.

The epic tale of William the Conqueror

Duke Robert, Richard II's son, had an illegitimate son, William, by a beautiful woman named Arlette. And it was William who finally succeeded in imposing his authority and peace throughout Normandy. He led an expeditionary force to fight the Duke of Brittany and, in doing so, sought the

1

1- The ramparts seen from the Great Outer Staircase. (Photograph by Bertrand Dauleux)

2- The abbey seen from north-east : the Marvel and the forework. (Photograph by Bertrand Dauleux)

3- The Great Inner Staircase seen from Gautier's Leap. (Photograph by Hervé Champollion)

2

3

assistance of the Saxon Count, Harold. The Bayeux Tapestry, which later retold the epic tale of William's life, shows the Duke crossing the R. Couesnon with his army. Behind him is Mont Saint-Michel - a building with two towers and a huge roof, standing on a platform at the top of the rock.

However, when William's cousin, Edward the Confessor, King of England, died, Harold seized the Crown. William prepared to invade England and he defeated his rival at Hastings in 1066 before going on to be crowned in Westminster. He came down to posterity as "William the Conqueror" and he united England and Normandy. In order to congratulate the victor, the Abbot of Mont Saint-Michel sent four monks whom William the Duke-King then appointed as advisers to his brother, Odo, Regent of England. Soon William designated his chaplain, Roger I (1085-1102), as Abbot of Mont Saint-Michel.

By the 11th century, Mont Saint-Michel had become a centre of intellectual excellence because, in order to be more effective in praying to God and to strengthen their faith, the monks needed holy texts or philosophical works concerned the Scriptures. This being so, manuscripts began to circulate from one monastery to another. They were then copied, illuminated i.e. illustrated, and annotated in the *scriptorium*, the copyists' workshop. Robert of Tombelaine annotated the *Canticle of Canticles*. The texts were also used to give greater beauty to ceremonies and they constituted one of the treasures of Benedictine abbeys.

Lanfranc, one of the most brilliant minds of the day, left Italy and came to live in Avranches. His presence caused intellectual ferment which soon spread to the nearby abbeys of Le Bec, founded by Hellouin the Knight, Lessay and Mont Saint-Michel. William made use of these erudite monks to control the Church in the country he had just conquered and Lanfranc became Archbishop of Canterbury. An abbey had, in fact, two functions. On the one hand, it was required to welcome monks frm other monasteries while on the other it was required to send monks to other lands as administrators, teachers and preachers.

The Christian world was eager for the supernatural in the 11th century and miracles became increasingly common. The monks took note of the events told by the pilgrims and all of them played a part in increasing the spiritual renown of Mont Saint-Michel.

One of them told how a young woman was trapped by the rising tide as she went into labour but the sea spared her life. Yet the most important miracle was the rediscovery of St. Aubert's bones. Divine music could be heard throughout the monastery, the monks bored holes into caskets and locks sprang open of their own accord. An unknown force even prostrated a disbelieving monk. Thereafter, the abbey had the relics of its founder, including a skull with a hole in it, a reminder of the Archangel's action.

Pilgrims came to the Mont to pray, and other Christians came to live there. Norgod, a Bishop of Avranches, saw the Mont haloed in a celestial light one night. He called it "St. Michael's light" and retired to the abbey. One of Normandy's great warriors, Néel de Saint-Sauveur, also came to the abbey to seek inner peace after a long life of battle.

Mont Saint-Michel at the height of its fame : the abbacy of Robert of Thorigny

The Mont became embroiled in quarrels among William's descendants relating to questions of succession. One of the Conqueror's sons, Henry Beauclerc, rebelled against his brothers, King William the Red of England and Duke Robert Curthose of Normandy. He shut himself in the monastery, since the Mont was also a citadel, but was finally obliged to surrender. He later took his revenge by becoming both King and Duke under the name of Henry I. His daughter married the Count of Anjou, Geoffrey Plantagenet. Their son, Henry, was Henry I's heir but the succession was contested. Mont Saint-Michel and Avranches were on opposing sides in this new civil war but Abbot Bernard du Bec (1131-1149) succeeded in imposing religious reform upon the Mont. He then put an end to the quarrels within the community and ordered the monks to go to Tombelaine on spiritual retreats. Henry II Plantagenet succeeded in re-establishing peace in the Duchy and in England, and by marrying Eleanor of Aquitaine he added a large part of France to these earlier territories.

The West Front. (Photograph by Bertrand Dauleux)

The church tower. (Photograph by Bertrand Dauleux)

The Romanesque nave in the minster. (Photograph by Bertrand Dauleux)

Henry II was delighted when Robert of Thorigny became Abbot, from 1154 to 1186. He also gained in importance as one of the Duke-King's advisers. Born into the nobility, Robert was first and foremost a historian and chronicler, who had already written a *"History of Henry I"*, Henry II's grandfather. He succeeded in bringing not only Bishops to the Mont but also Henry II himself. After signing a peace treaty with King Louis VII of France, the two monarchs came to Mont Saint-Michel with their Court. Rarely had such a procession been seen here before - nor was it again afterwards.

The Abbot of Mont Saint-Michel became increasingly involved in the Duchy's politics and in the main events that befell Henry II's family. In 1170, the King let his courtiers murder Thomas à Becket, Archbishop of Canterbury, in his own cathedral.

Robert de Thorigny was an ecclesiastic but he was also the King's man and he made strenuous efforts to reconcile the Church and the sovereign. It was he who prepared the King's symbolic act of penitence on the steps in front of Avranches Cathedral. Thanks to this prudence, Robert de Thorigny's influence spread within the Church and throughout the Christian world.

Robert also set up a school on Mont Saint-Michel to train novices in music and poetry. One of these novices, William of Saint-Pair, was a troubadour, writing his poem, *"Roman du Mont Saint-Michel*, in the Romance language and not in Latin.

Finally, Robert extended the abbey and a hostelry was built on the south side of the monastery to welcome pilgrims. These buildings collapsed in the early years of the 19th century. For himself, the Abbot had austere apartments built on the west side. He also had two towers built on the West Front of the church.

The abbacy of Robert de Thorigny was Mont Saint-Michel's finest hour politically, materially and intellectually. It also marked the end of an era - the age of Romanesque architecture and the reign of the Dukes.

The King of France becomes Protector of the monastery and the Marvel is built

After the death of Richard the Lionheart in 1199, King Philip Augustus of France took advantage of the weak dynasty in England to conquer Normandy. Mont Saint-Michel, though, remained loyal to England and found itself at the centre of the war, attacked by one of France's allies, Guy de Thouars. The monks put up strong resistance but a fire destroyed a large number of houses in the village and part of the abbey, in 1203. After his victory at the Battle of Bouvines, Philip became the uncontested master of Normandy but was then faced with the need to win the loyalty and esteem of his subjects in the region. He sent the abbot a large sum of money to pay for the rebuilding of the abbey. Philip's grandson, Louis IX, the future St. Louis, came to Mont Saint-Michel in 1256 and laid a bag of gold coins on the High Altar. This money was used to build fortifications. Then, in 1311, Philip the Fair came to the island on a pilgrimage. All these royal visits established the sovereign, who represented temporal power, as protector of the abbey. However, this authority was far away, and the King of France, unlike the Dukes of Normandy, took little part in the internal life of the community or the election of the Abbot.

At the end of the 12th century, successive abbots decided to build new accommodation for the monks on the north side of the abbey. The brothers had tired of the dark, narrow Romanesque chambers and wanted more space and more light. They also wanted a more attractive setting for their everyday life. Three storeys of vast chambers were therefore built during the first forty years of the 13th century, the chambers that we now know as the Marvel. This was the period of major building projects throughout Europe, the building of the great cathedrals, and Mont Saint-Michel played its part in developping an architectural style that was later to be called "Gothic".

This enormous mass of stone had to be shored up, lightened and supported. Huge piers leaning against the rough walls of rock were used as supports. Pillars and vaulting supported each of the three storeys. Technical innovation had resulted in a building that was as architecturally successful as it was aesthetically beautiful. The masterpiece was completed by elegant decorative features, especially in the cloisters.

The three storeys on the eastern side were the first to be built. From bottom to top, they included

The abbey seen from the south-west. (Photograph by Hervé Champollion)

The abbey seen from the west, with the Marvel and the church. (Photograph by Hervé Champollion)

the almonry, the Guests' Chamber and the refectory. They were followed by the western side, with the undercroft, Knights' Chamber and cloisters. A third section was planned but never built. The layout of the Marvel was rational, and respected the double purpose of the abbey viz. the monks' life of prayer and accommodation for pilgrims. The area reserved for the monks, the enclosure, consisted of the refectory and cloisters at the top of the building. On the western side of the intermediate floor, was the so-called Knights' Chamber, in fact the calefactory or work room. On the lower floor was the undercroft, again part of the monks' everyday life since it was here that they stored their food, while the adjacent almonry accommodated the poorest of pilgrims, for whom the almoner could take supplies from the undercroft. Above the almonry, on the intermediate level, was the Guests' Chamber, designed for VIP visitors. They were nearer the monks, who worked in the adjacent room. This meant that such guests were allowed to come into closer contact with the life of the community. In fact, the architecture was a reflection of society as a whole, an image of mediaeval hierarchy. On the bottom rung of the ladder were the poor, above them was the nobility, and at the top were the men of the Church.

When the monastery buildings were being erected, the community was going through a difficult period in its history. The Benedictines had been criticised by other Orders in the Western world, firstly by the Cistercians who criticised them for having abandoned manual labour and secondly by the Mendicant Orders that criticised their wealth and attention to material comforts. On Mont Saint-Michel, there was often an atmosphere of acute crisis. Despite this, however, the abbots succeeded in imposing their will and, in the end, it was the Archangel who saved the Mont, since the monks were obliged to avoid any hint of scandal and provide pilgrims with decent accommodation because it was their gifts that enabled the abbey to exist and prosper.

From Matins to Compline : everyday life on Mont Saint-Michel

The monks (they numbered approximately sixty during the abbacy of Robert of Thorigny) had regained the power to elect their Abbot but the chosen candidate had to promise loyalty to the King of France, swear obedience to the Bishop of Avranches and undertake to respect the monastery's customs i.e. the monks' rights. The professed monks (those who had taken their vows) met in the "chapter" to discuss the abbey's affairs. At the end of the Middle Ages, the Abbot was often absent and the monastic community acquired enormous independence. In addition to the professed brothers, most of whom came from aristocratic families, there were the lay brothers of more modest origin, who undertook the domestic chores, and the novices who were preparing for monastic life. In addition to the brothers, there was a large group of servants and guards.

The day was broken up by the eight canonical hours (Matins, Lauds, Prime, Tierce, Sext, Nones, Vespers, and Compline) and two grand Masses. In the minster, the monks sat in the chancel while the pilgrims prayed in the nave. However, the entire monastery could be used for religious ceremony - cloisters and crypts, great staircases and nave alike.

The Benedictines were particularly careful to vary and embellish the worship of God. When at prayer, they left off their black habits and wore their long, white, ceremonial albs. Religious feastdays were also given added significance through the candles, holy water and incense, Crucifixes and all the other objects used in worship, the dais, the gold of the reliquaries, the Gospels and the illuminated manuscripts, and the statues of the Saints. But the essential part of any service remained prayer, according to the rules of plainsong. The celebration of the divine word even gave rise to veritable playlets akin to dramatic productions - mystery plays.

Life on Mont Saint-Michel meant accepting geographical isolation, on a rock in the midst of the waves. The abbey was, to an extent, self-sufficient. It ensured that it had sufficient food, tanks were built to provide the water supply, the ill were cared for on the island, and the novices received their education there. Yet the community remained in touch with events in the outside world through the influx of pilgrims. As years passed, the Benedictines became increasingly concerned with their creature comforts. Indeed, they had a tendency to forget the Rule and allow themselves forms of luxury.

An aerial view of Mont Saint-Michel.

God's walkers en route for Mont Saint-Michel

Pilgrims were attracted to Mont Saint-Michel very early on in its history, through worship of St. Michael. They came in increasing numbers after the abbey was founded in 966 A.D. and during the Crusades, since a Crusade was also a pilgrimage to a holy city, Jerusalem. Although Mont Saint-Michel was first and foremost a centre of pilgrimage for Normans and Bretons, it also attracted believers from all over Europe. And the worship of the Archangel gained in popularity after the Mont had successfully withstood attack by the English during the One Hundred Years' War.

Travellers came to the monastery to pray, to thank God for His goodness or to fulfil a vow. But pilgrims also sought forgiveness for their sins. A pilgrimage could even be the punishment meted out by a court of justice. It could also be a means of seeking a cure for a disease, illness or disability.

Pilgrims equiped themselves with a special staff with a knot in the middle and a crozier at the top, and with a leather pouch. They were also easily recognisable by their clothes, which included a voluminous cloak. They followed the "Mont" paths, also known as the Ways to Heaven, and five main roads converged on Mont Saint-Michel. But pilgrims could be beset by any number of dangers including brigands, epidemics, or war. Because of this, there were inns along the road, as well as hospices for the sick. The final stage involved the crossing of the shore at low tide, and this in itself was often a dangerous thing to do. Yet huge numbers of people crowded onto Mont Saint-Michel for major ceremonies, especially as Christians in those days were very fond of marvels and went in search of sources of wonderment.

The relics formed the basis of the pilgrims' veneration since they were supposed to have miraculous powers. Travellers would make an offering to St. Michael and, before leaving the Mont, would choose a souvenir such as a cockleshell, or a pilgrim's badge. These lead or tin objects were sewn onto the pilgrims' clothes and represented the Archangel.

Early in the 14th century, pilgrimages for children and adolescents became increasingly popular. These children's "Crusades" were also adolescent festivals, but they resulted in public disorder since valets, apprentices and tramps mingled with the young people. The young pilgrims were known as "*pastoureaux*", the name given to young shepherd lads and lasses. Some of the children were very young indeed (no more than eight years old), and some travelled vast distances, from the banks of the Rhine or the South of France. They were led by students and processed behind the banners of their area, all bearing a picture of St. Michael. Sometimes they set off against their parents' wishes and remained absent for a long time. Even if they received assistance along the way, they often suffered from extreme fatigue and disease. Some of them died. The political and religious authorities of the day disliked these phenomena but the children's pilgrimages continued to exist until the outbreak of the French Revolution.

Mont Saint-Michel, a symbol of resistance during the One Hundred Years' War

War between France and England seemed imminent from the early 14th century onwards. Along with the plague that spread throughout the Christian world, the country was ravaged by fighting. This was the so-called One Hundred Years' War. After French defeats at Poitiers and Crécy, there was some reversal of the situation thanks to the leadership of King Charles V assisted by Bertrand Du Guesclin, a Breton knight who was Captain of Pontorson. When, later, he left France for Spain, the future Constable of France entrusted his wife, Tiphaine, to the care of the Archangel.

Tiphaine's house was at the top end of the town. She spent her time there doing good works and learning about her favourite subject, astrology.

Abbot Pierre Le Roi made the fortification of the abbey his top priority, and the entrance to the monastery was defended by towers and ramparts, forming the forework and its barbican. He also completed the abbey lodgings on the south side of the Mont. The lodgings included the Abbot's apartments and the administrative and legal services. Charles VI, the King who ended life insane, came to Mont Saint-

1

2

1- The Flamboyant Gothic chancel.
(Photograph by Hervé Champollion)
2- The north side of the Romanesque nave (12th century). (Photograph by Hervé Champollion)
3- The abbey's coat-of-arms.
(Photograph by Bertrand Dauleux)
4- The chevet. (Photograph by Bertrand Dauleux)

3

4

Michel on a pilgrimage. He appointed Pierre Le Roi, who was also a well-known university teacher, his adviser for ecclesiastical matters, at the time when the Church was being turned upside down by the great Schism of the Western World and the confrontation between two Popes.

Normandy fell into enemy hands in 1415, after the disastrous French defeat at Agincourt. The Duke of Bedford, the brother of the English monarch, was appointed governor of the province and he rallied a number of major Norman personalities to his cause. Among them was Robert Jolivet, successor to Pierre Le Roi, who accepted a position as adviser to Bedford and, in reward, was given all the monastery's wealth.

The monks refused to follow their abbot's lead and betray France. Knights who had been dispossessed of their lands had sought protection in the monastery. They remained faithful to the French cause, whose only defender was the Heir Apparent, Charles, later King Charles VII, who had taken refuge in Bourges.

On Mont Saint-Michel, the Romanesque chancel in the church collapsed and the war made any attempt at rebuilding impossible. Like a sinister warning, the R. Couesnon changed its course in 1420 after a particularly high tide and flowed between Mont Saint-Michel and Tombelaine. The smaller island soon fell into English hands and they set up a garrison there.

The victors decided to demolish the fortress-island that was withstanding attack, but a citadel well-defended by its ramparts and the sea was impregnable. It would have to be encircled and be forced to surrender when food supplies ran out. The siege began in 1424. Numerous troops were stationed around the Bay. A small wooden fortress called the "bastille" was built in Ardevon opposite the Mont in order to keep watch on the shoreline. As a final measure, a small flotilla of ships provided a blockade out to sea. An expeditionary force of Breton noblemen set off from Saint-Malo; skilful seafarers launched an attack on the English ships and dispersed them. This naval victory made it possible to get supplies of food into the Mont by sea. The total blockade had failed and the citadel had not surrendered.

This success was the first enjoyed by the French camp for a long time and it gave the French back their confidence. The Archangel seemed to have been instrumental in allowing the event to take place and he gained renewed prestige. This is why St. Michael was one of the angels who appeared to Joan of Arc, saying "I am Michael, protector of France, arise and go to assist the King of France". And he guided the shepherd girl from Lorraine throughout her epic journey. In fact, the adventures of the Maid of Orleans bear some resemblance to certain children's pilgrimages.

A skilful captain named Louis d'Estouteville was appointed by Charles VII to take charge of the garrison on Mont Saint-Michel. He tried to put an end to the quarrels, conspiracies, and debauchery that were rife in the abbey, for the men of war had introduced all the excesses of their own lifestyle. This renewed grasp on authority enabled the citadel to withstand the final English attack in 1433. Fire broke out in the town, the timber houses were destroyed and the ramparts were damaged. The English sought to take advantage of the situation and approached the island in large numbers, supported by awesome artillery that opened a breach in the walls. The enemies thought the town had been taken but the garrison clung on and the attackers were forced to retreat. The knights on the Mont recovered two enormous bombards that were set up at the entrance to the town, where they can still be seen today.

The town had been protected by a ring of ramparts and massive towers. There again, the defenders of the Mont showed enormous imagination. They were aware of the new type of warfare and the role of artillery. Round towers proved to be particularly susceptible to damage under cannon fire and so, when constructing the Buckle Tower, Louis d'Estouteville selected a polygonal shape that provided greater resistance. This was the bastion design that was to spread throughout the Western World and, in the 15th century, the Buckle Tower was one of the earliest examples of it. Vauban later brought the design to the peak of perfection. Thanks to the war, Mont Saint-Michel had become one of the most redoubtable fortresses of its day.

The Knights of St. Michael

Louis d'Estouteville enjoyed such enormous prestige that he was able to impose his brother, Guillaume d'Estouteville, as Abbot of Mont Saint-Michel. This choice marked a twofold historical change. Firstly, the King of France was granted, by the Pope, the right to appoint bishops and certain abbots who were no longer elected. Secondly, an abbey could be given to a cleric (or even, in some

The Crypt of the Mighty Pillars. (Photograph by Bertrand Dauleux)
St. Martin's Chapel (inset). (Photograph by Bertrand Dauleux)

cases, to a lay person) and not to a monk, and the abbot was no longer resident in the community. He merely received the lion's share of the income. This was the commendatory system which enabled the sovereign to reward an adviser, a courtier or a great nobleman. Cardinal Guillaume did not forget his monastery though. He obtained indulgences which encouraged pilgrimages. And the rebuilding of the chancel began with the Crypt of the Mighty Pillars. The Cardinal also instigated proceedings aimed at rehabilitating Joan of Arc, thereby atoning for Robert Jolivet who had been one of the judges who passed judgement on the Maid of Orleans.

Louis XI came to the Mont twice. The House of France, like the other dynasties in Europe, wanted to invent its own order of chivalry. As St. Michael had been instrumental in helping the French to defeat the English, Louis XI gathered round his august person the "Knights of St. Michael", whom he selected from among the grandest noblemen in the land. Their dress included a collar with a medallion depicting the Archangel slaying the dragon, a motto *Immensi tremor oceani* (the terror of the immense ocean), and several seashells.

Louis XI also had another, more lugubrious idea. He was a heartless monarch who had one of his "daughters" installed on the Mont. It was a wooden cage hung from the ceiling and was used to imprison offenders. Every time the occupant moved, the cage rocked. The lack of space and total solitude were a form of torture.

The rebuilding of the chancel in the minster was completed early in the 16th century. In this part of the church, verticality was given precedence. The pillars, devoid of capitals and the narrow spans underline the impression of an "upthrust" and a surge skywards. With the prismatic ribs on the vaulted roof, the stone lacework in the triforium, the traceried gallery, and the forest of carved stone on the chevet, mediaeval architecture had found its final dazzling expression on the Mont, through a style known as Flamboyant Gothic.

Decline in more modern times

During the Renaissance, the abbey found itself far removed from the new centres of artistic life and political power, and monasteries were no longer considered as beacons of civilisation. Yet two Kings of France, François I and Charles IX, still made a pilgrimage to Mont Saint-Michel with their courtiers. The rock also remained a fortress and was still at stake in fighting during the Wars of Religion. The Protestants sought to capture it, because it was one of the strongholds of the League, a Catholic extremist organisation. The Mont was subject to no less than nine attacks from 1577 to 1598.

The Abbots were chosen from among the great families in the kingdom such as Cossé, Guise, and Montmorency-Laval, but they seldom came to the Mont. Yet it was one of these commendatory abbots who imposed a change on the lifestyle of Mont Saint-Michel's monks. They had been leading a worldly life and the abbey was falling into decline. During the abbacy of Guise, it was decided to bring in monks from a new Benedictine Order, the Maurists. They arrived in 1622 and were living proof of the major shake-up that was to mark the Catholic Church in the 17th century. They devoted their life to study.

They saved the archives, studied them carefully and, in some cases, became historians. Among these erudite monks were Dom Jean Huysnes and Dom Thomas Le Roy. The community's resources, however, did not allow them to maintain the huge buildings, which gradually fell into disrepair. Tastes had changed and mediaeval architecture, which was disdainfully described as "Gothic" i.e. barbarous, was no longer popular. When spans collapsed in the church, a Classical West Front was built as an end wall. It was completed in 1780.

Like many other monasteries, the one on Mont Saint-Michel had long been a prison and the monks looked after "our gentleman exiles". Some of these exiles were sent to the Mont after receiving a *lettre de cachet*, a royal sentence not open to appeal, usually handed down for affairs of State that required absolute secrecy. Ecclesiastics were exiled to Mont Saint-Michel, as were a number of persons deemed guilty of debauchery.

The future King Louis-Philippe, the Duke of Orleans' son, came to visit Mont Saint-Michel in 1788 with his brothers and they ordered the destruction of the cage invented by Louis XI, this "monument of barbarity".

The French Revolution led to the dissolution of religious Orders but did nothing to change the Mont's awesome purpose as a prison. All types of political opponents were sent here. There were

1

1- The cloisters are on the upper storey on the west side of the Marvel. (Photograph by Bertrand Dauleux)

2- The gallery in the cloisters
(Photograph by Bertrand Dauleux)

3- The colonettes in the cloisters.
(Photograph by Hervé Champollion)

3

2

priests and Royalist rebels, and Babeuf, the leader of the Conspiracy of Equals. Then every new revolution, riot, or conspiracy sent new detainees to the island. Among them were Barbès, a Republican, and Blanqui, the eternal prisoner. Colombat, a well-known artist, managed to escape; Barbès did not.

In 1863, Mont Saint-Michel ceased to be a prison. Romantic writers had brought mediaeval art and architecture back into fashion and the Mont delighted them because of its subtle beauty. In 1874, the abbey and ramparts became "listed buildings" and restoration work began. When the monastery celebrated the one thousand years of its existence in 1966, one monk came back to the Mont, quickly followed by a small community.

Visiting Mont Saint-Michel

When visitors arrive at the foot of Mont Saint-Michel, they pass through three gates - the **Forward Gate**, the **Boulevard Gate** and, finally, the **King's Gate**. The town entrance was particularly well-guarded for it was the weak point of any fortress. The English bombards are there to serve as reminders of the long siege withstood by the people of the Mont during the One Hundred Years' War.

The main street leads up to the abbey on top of the rock. A vast staircase known as the **Great Outer Staircase** leads from the village to the monastery. Here again, the entrance is particularly well-defended, firstly by a forework, a crenelated defensive structure, and then by the barbican with its two turrets. But the walls of the abbey itself formed veritable ramparts with the massive Gothic Marvel on the north side and the succession of lodgings to the south. The Guardroom serves as a reminder that the Mont had a military purpose throughout its history.

The **Great Inner Staircase** leads from the Guardroom to a terrace known as **Gautier's Leap.**

The minster

Visitors reach the minster by the West terrace high above the sea. It was built to replace the spans in the Romanesque nave that had collapsed. The 18th-century **Classical West Front** is a particularly austere piece of architecture. The tower was rebuilt in the late 19th century in accordance with the precepts of Romanesque architecture and given a Gothic spire, a copy of the one on Notre-Dame Cathedral in Paris. On top of the spire is a statue of Michael, the Archangel, slaying the dragon. It was made by Frémiet and put the finishing touch to the outline of Mont Saint-Michel as we see it today.

Inside the church is a shield reminiscent of the abbey's coat-of-arms, with shells that symbolise pilgrimages and fleurs-de-lys symbolising the protection of the King of France.

The **Romanesque nave** could hold crowds of pilgrims and was built in two stages, in the 11th and 12th centuries. Columns backing onto the walls served as inner piers while huge pillars provided support for the timber beams that were lighter than stone vaulting. Side aisles were then built to support the immense nave broken up horizontally by spans and, vertically, by three storeys - the great arches, the galleries and the clerestory. As to the arms of the transept, they were given semi-circular vaulting laid out in such a way as to counterbalance the transept crossing. The Romanesque chancel collapsed later in the abbey's history.

At the end of the 15th century, the original chancel was replaced by the **Flamboyant Gothic chancel** which includes the same three storeys as in the nave but in this instance it is the overall sense of verticality which is given priority. The triforium was the original decorative feature. The openwork gallery was designed to let light into the building. With its arches and slender ribbed vaulting (or lancets), it is a piece of veritable lacework in stone. An ambulatory ran round the chancel so that the faithful could attend the services.

In order to support the particularly high vaulting in the chancel, flying buttresses were added to columns and walls outside the minster. Seen as a whole, the **chevet** forms a quarter sphere in which the decorative genius of the so-called Flamboyant Gothic architecture led to the inclusion of a plethora of pinnacles, stone pyramids decorated with finials or stone flowers.

The **lace stairway** gives access to the top of the chevet, from which there is a panoramic view of the entire Bay.

1

1- The monks' refectory is on the upper storey on the east side of the Marvel. (Photograph by Bertrand Dauleux)

2- The Guests' Chamber is on the intermediate storey on the east side of the Marvel. (Photograph by Bertrand Dauleux)

3- The Gothic almonry is on the lower storey. (Photograph by Bertrand Dauleux)

2

3

The Romanesque abbey buildings and the crypts

On the north side of the church, but on the same level, was the monks' dorter. On the lower level was the **Chapel of Our Lady of the Thirty Candles**, the crypt which supported the north arm of the transept and was dedicated to the Virgin Mary. The **Monk's Gallery** is a fine chamber with ribbed vaulting.

The Romanesque almonry beneath it has been given the name "Aquilon Chamber". It lay near the entrance to the Romanesque abbey and was the first room entered by pilgrims. It was given groined vaulting, a foretaste of the ribbed vaulting to come.

The techniques used for vaulted roofs improved and gained in diversity. Semi-circular barrel vaulting was heavy and could, therefore, only be of limited size. By crossing two semi-circular vaults at right angles to each other, the architects obtained groined vaulting. But it had a tendency to become misshapen and the groins were replaced by stone ribs that were cut and then carefully adjusted to fit. They cut through each other and balanced the building as a whole, since they were supported on pillars. This meant that only the stone outline was of any importance. Ribbed vaulting enabled architects to produce larger, more flexible designs, and paved the way for the prowesses of the Gothic era.

Robert de Thorigny had his modest **apartments** built to the west of the abbey, slightly away from the monks' quarters. Beneath the apartments were two dungeons dug into the rock. They were given the nickname "the twins".

Our Lady Underground is the Preromanesque church that was later turned into a crypt. The abbey then extended southwards with the buildings used to accommodate pilgrims but this hostelry collapsed in the early 19th century. A large treadwheel was installed nearby. Men used to walk round inside it and heave a trolley along a hoist, a sort of stone ladder snaking its way up the rock face.

St. Martin's Crypt supports the south arm of the transept. Its barrel vault is a model of austere rigour. The **Crypt of the Mighty Pillars** was built in the late Middle Ages, from 1446 to 1450, to provide support for the new chancel. Ten enormous pillars were built, two of them reminiscent of palm trees.

The Gothic Marvel

On the upper storey, the **cloisters** were used by the monks for exercise and conversation. The small garden at the top of the rock is flanked by galleries with a timber roof supported on pink granite colonettes set out in staggered rows. This sequence of tripods ensures that the construction is particularly stable. Above, between the arches, are subtly-carved soft Caen limestone squinches, on which the plant theme predominates. The carvings stand out against a background in shade. Some of the squinches are decorated with figures such as the Paschal Lamb, Chirst, and St. Francis of Assissi. On the south wall was the **lavatorium** with its double bench and fountain. This was where the Abbot washed the monks' feet, in memory of Christ washing His disciples' feet. The three bays were originally designed to lead into the third section of the Marvel, the chapter house, but it was never built. In the north-west corner is the charter house where the abbey kept its charters, or archives.

The **refectory** on the same level was used by the monks, who ate in silence. One of the brothers would read from holy texts. The reader's pulpit is built into the south wall and the reader's voice filled the entire chamber thanks to the excellent acoustics. Instead of using a stone vaulted roof, which would have been too heavy, the architects preferred a timber roof that resembles a huge upturned hull. The tall, narrow openings, almost slit-windows, flanked by colonettes cannot be seen from the doorway yet they allow light to pour into the room without weakening the thick walls.

On the second storey of the Marvel is the **Knights' Chamber** where the monks worked and studied. Its name serves as a reminder of the Order of Chivalry founded by Louis XI. This was also the **scriptorium**, the workshop where the copyists and illuminators worked. The huge fireplaces provided a source of heat for the chamber, hence its name of "calefactory". Wide windows provided maximum light, a vital feature for the monks' work. The robust pillars are decorated with foliage and support fine ribbed vaulting. Latrines were built behind the fireplaces.

To the east side of the same storey is the **Guests' Room** which was used as a reception room for any august visitors to the abbey. It contains two aisles in which the tables were set out, two vast fireplaces where the food was prepared, and latrines in the north wall. These elements constituted all the necessary "mod. cons" for a reception room. The elegance of the ribbed vaulting and columns, the light that

The Knight's Chamber is on the intermediate level of the Marvel, on the west side. (Photograph by Bertrand Dauleux)

The undercroft is on the lower storey of the Marvel. (Photograph by Bertrand Dauleux)

floods in through the great bay windows, and the beauty of the stylised foliage turned Gothic architecture into a style worthy of ceremonial. This is one of the most elegant pieces of vernacular architecture built in the Middle Ages. In the neighbouring St. Madeleine's Chapel, visitors could pray before and after meals.

The lower storey contains the **undercroft** and **almonry**, two rooms of immense, robust simplicity. A bay and a ramp were included in the design to facilitate the arrival of food in the undercroft. The almonry was used to accommodate the poorest pilgrims.

The **Corbies,** *or* **Crows, Tower** on the south-east corner of the Marvel provided access from one storey to another. It was topped by a pyramid-shaped stone roof.

Above the Guardroom was **Belle-Chaise,** which got its name (literally "Fine Chair") from the throne installed on the orders of Abbot Pierre Le Roi. It was here that the abbot meted out justice.

This chamber was part of the **abbey lodgings** on the south side of the abbey, which constituted the Abbot's Palace.

The town and its ramparts

The small Norman village nestles at the foot of the abbey to which it has always been linked. In days gone by, pilgrims found inns and taverns there, and could buy their pilgrimage badges. A few of the old houses have survived, like the Arcade House, the Artichoke House, or the Unicorn Hostelry; others, like the building known as Tiphaine de Raguenel's House, have been restored. As to Old Mother Poulard, whose real name was Anne Poulard, she gained a reputation for her hospitality and her omelettes.

The parish church was dedicated to St. Peter.

The town was protected by its ramparts and visitors should not miss a walk round them. The **North Tower** is the highest; the **Buckle Tower** the most unusual. The section of town wall running from the Buckle Tower to the King's Gate was built early in the 15th century during the One Hundred Years' War, before the long siege of Mont Saint-Michel. The **Gabriel Tower** gets its name from the engineer Gabriel Dupuy who ordered it to be built. A windmill was set up on the platform in the 17th century. It protected the Hayloft Enclosure, where the abbey had its storerooms. At the foot of the rock lies **St. Aubert's Spring**.

Main characteristics

Length of dyke to Mont : 1 mile. Circumference of Mont : 1/2 mile.

Height of abbey above sea level : 255 ft.

Size of Archangel : base to sword : 14 1/2 ft.

Archangel : 9 ft ; weight : almost 9 cwt.

The town seen from the chevet of the church.
(Photograph by Hervé Champollion)

The Artichoke House.
(Photograph by Hervé Champollion)

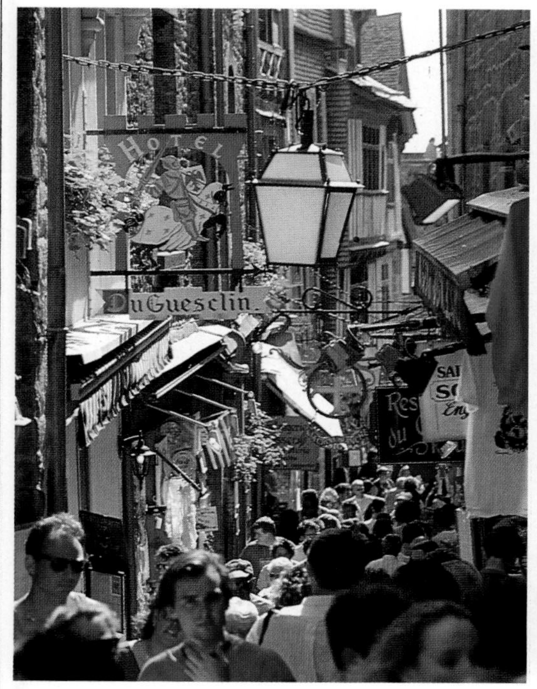

The Grand-Rue. (Photograph by F. Hamon/Andia)

The parish church and graveyard. (Photograph by Hervé Boulé)

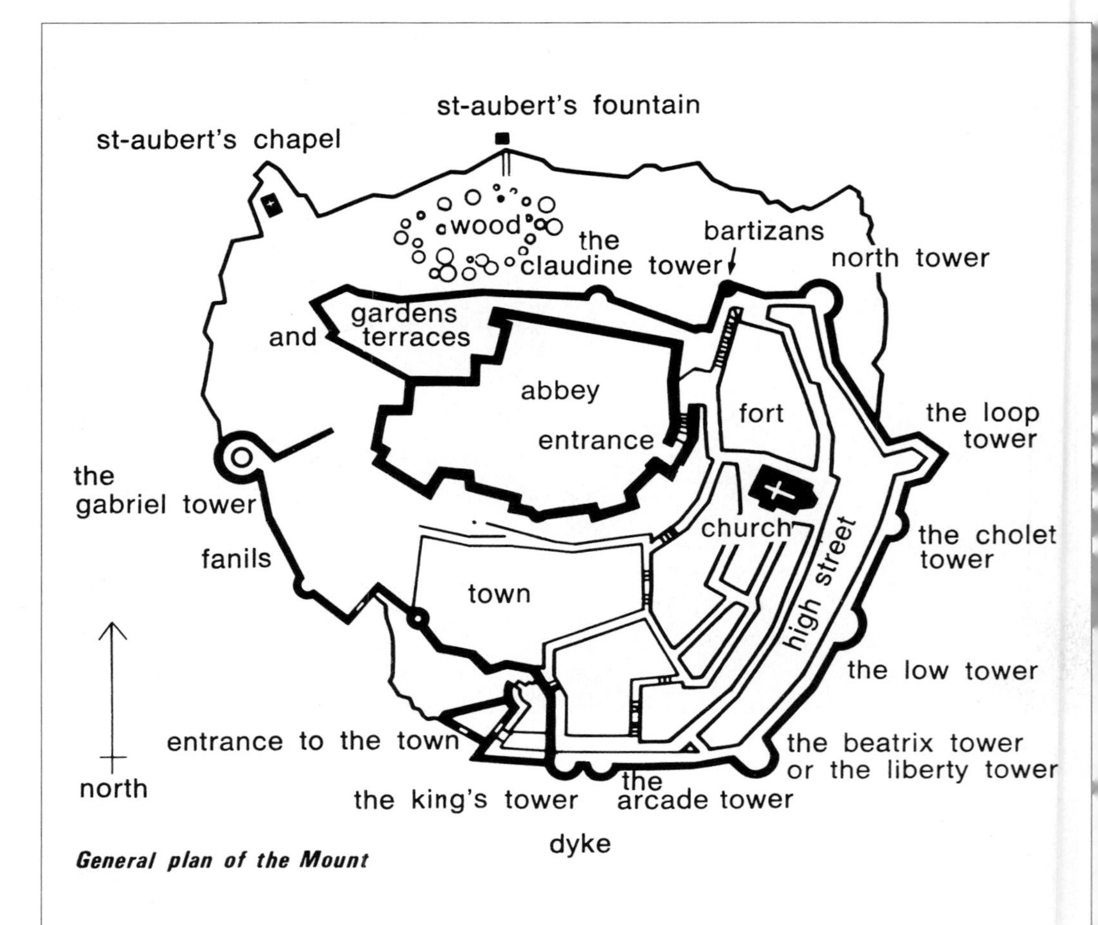

General plan of the Mount

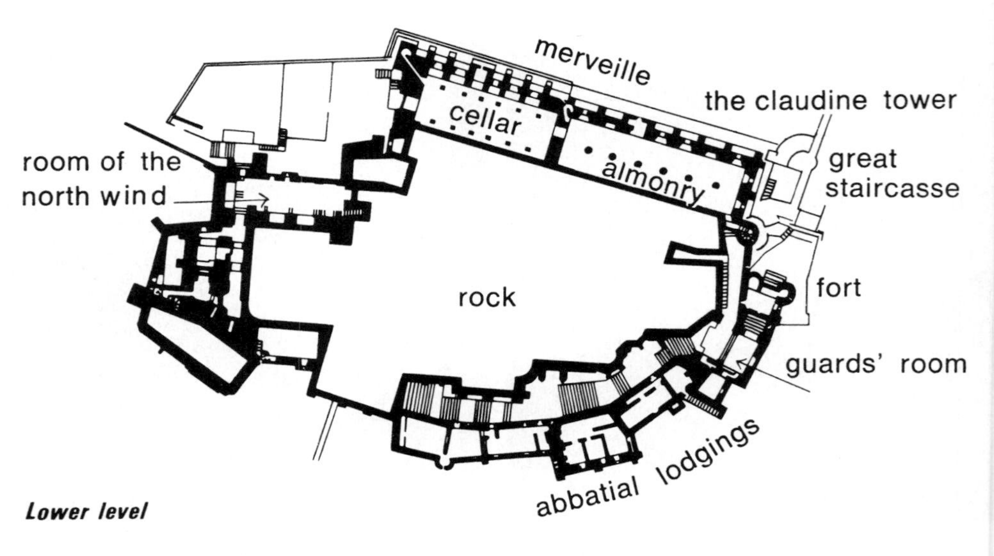

Lower level

The great tread wheel. (Photograph by Hervé Champollion)

The North Tower. (Photograph by Bertrand Dauleux)

The town walls. (Photograph by Bertrand Dauleux)

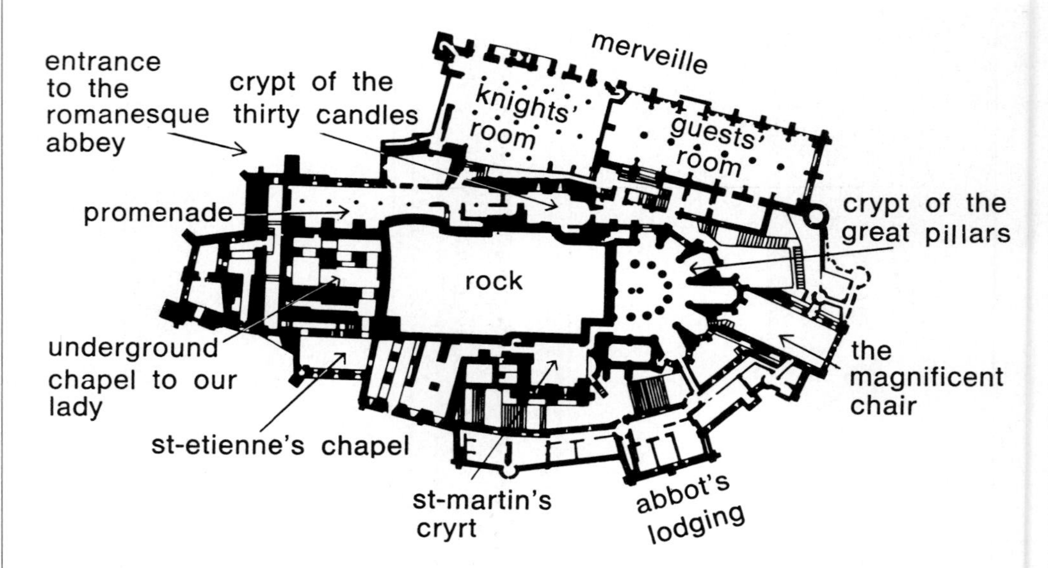

Middle level

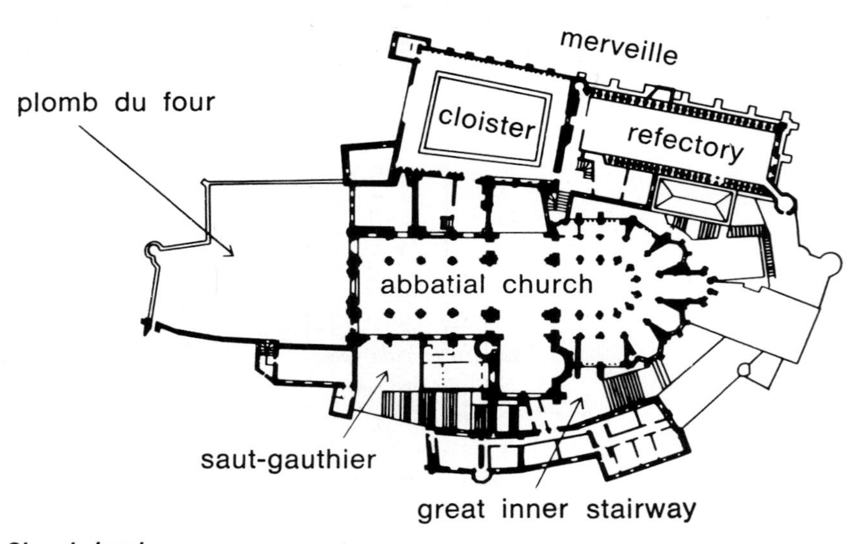

Church level

Frontispiece : The silhouette of the Mont Saint-Michel. (Photograph by Hervé Champollion)
Frontispiece : The mass. (Photograph by Hervé Champollion)
Back cover : The Gothic chancel. (Photograph by Hervé Champollion)

 I.S.B.N 2 7373.1553.0 - Dépôt légal : avril 1994 - N° d'éditeur : 2942.04.06.01.97
Imprimerie Raynard, La Guerche-de-Bretagne (35).